Confidence

For LIFE!

23 Proven Strategies to Increase YOUR Confidence

For Greater Success!

Dave Williams

ISBN: 9798352496688

Confidence *For* LIFE!

23 Proven Strategies to Increase YOUR Confidence
For Greater Success!

Dave Williams

WHAT OTHERS ARE SAYING ABOUT
DAVE WILLIAMS AND HIS STRATEGIES

"Dave, I cannot thank you enough as I sailed through the interview I had today. Thank you for all your help with my confidence as it felt amazing!"
- Helen Hughes
Manager

"When it comes to working with an executive coach, there are many to choose from, however, I made the right choice when I decided to work with Dave. Dave took the time to understand what I needed and showed himself to be both observant and an excellent listener. He has a wealth of knowledge and experience, which he is able to relay in a way you feel encouraged and ready to use. I am most impressed with his energy and focus, so much so, I look forward to when I am speaking with him next. Having worked with Dave for just a few weeks, already I feel much more confident and better able to deal with challenges in work and in my personal life too."
- Loraine Thomas
HR Director

"Dave, thanks for not being patronising, and for buckling me into the driving seat, and showing me how to get to my destination."
- Paula Wollaston
Senior Manager

"Excellent course and training. Dave was a great trainer providing a lot of valuable advice to help us improve. A very worthwhile decision."
- Max Dixon
Director

"Out of all the training courses I've attended and trainers I've met so far, you've been the most inspiring."
- Anna Bailey
Business Owner

"Dave, without hesitation, you have been the best guest speaker we have ever had!"
- **Bosco Bonilla**
Provost, Universidad Americana, Nicaragua

"Dave's commitment and caring are outstanding. He has the ability to listen deeply and then ask the right questions to enable you to find the solutions you need. Dave offers amazing tools to enable you to make changes and find a new direction. Thanks Dave xxx!"
- **Kay Hebborn**
Business Owner, Canada

"I must say," I do like what you do" and the way you take the audience on a thought-provoking journey of self-exploration, and discovery. Very difficult to do what you do and do it well (which you did), where people after your session felt empowered. Thank you again for sharing your experiences and bringing light into the room."
- **Ron Lawrence, MBE**

"Just a quick note to say thank you for all your help and assistance yesterday. There were several 'lightbulb moments' that will see a massive change in my approach. I think over time I have built some blockers up that meant I could not see the wood through the trees!"
- **Paul Jenkins**
Academy Manager

"Thanks Dave, that's the first time in ages I've managed to get clarity about where I am headed."
- **Ian James**
CEO

"Thank you from the bottom of my heart for helping turn my mum's life around. She's had so many years of pain to deal with, and now I've got my mum back."
- **Manny Bahra**
A grateful son

"I can't thank you enough! I have been going through a challenging time recently with both work and my personal life and didn't know why I wasn't performing as I should have been. After getting together on Friday, I didn't realise I had been behaving the way I had and now I feel liberated thanks to you and am looking forward to changing things around."
- **Tony Wilson**
Business Owner

"Having met several coaches over the years, Dave is the first one who really gets and understands me and is not afraid of asking the difficult questions to help me move forward."
- **James Jones**
CEO

"You're a star! Words can't sum up how supportive and kind you are, and all the support you have given me overall this ongoing saga. Your advice and insight has made a huge difference!"
- **Jane Morgan MBE**

"Dave is the most compassionate Coach I know. He has a heart of gold! The quality of your life and the quality of your work will be improved because of Dave Williams and his coaching. He has the knack of getting to the core of your problem in a way that makes it so easy to make the changes you want to make and move forward with your life. If you're feeling stuck, get Dave!"
- **James Lavers - the "Guru Maker"**
Developing leading lights in the fields of personal, professional & spiritual development for 20 years. www.jameslavers.com

N.B. Some of the names have been changed to protect my client's privacy

MOTIVATE AND INSPIRE OTHERS!

"Share this book"

Retail £25.00

Special Quantity

5 – 20 Books	£10.99
21 – 99 Books	£9.99
100 – 499 Books	£8.99
500 – 999 Books	£7.99
1000+ Books	£6.99

To place an order contact:

dave@davewilliamscoaching.com

THE IDEAL PROFESSIONAL SPEAKER FOR YOUR NEXT EVENT!

Any organisation that wants to develop their people to become "extraordinary," needs to hire Dave Williams for a keynote and/or workshop training.

TO CONTACT OR BOOK
Dave Williams
TO SPEAK

dave@davewilliamscoaching.com

www.switchonthelightcoach.co.uk

THE IDEAL COACH FOR YOU!

If you're ready to overcome challenges, have major breakthroughs and achieve higher levels, then you will love having Dave Williams as your coach!

TO CONTACT OR BOOK:
Dave Williams

dave@davewilliamscoaching.com

www.confidencecoach.uk

DEDICATION

It is with respect, admiration, and sincere appreciation, that I dedicate this book to Helen and her mum, Bet. Without you and the lessons you taught me, I would not have the blessing of being where I am today. Thank you from the bottom of my heart! I love you dearly!

Helen, 'Hel'

Bet, a lovely, brave, funny lady

CONFIDENCE
- AN INTRODUCTION

Why is it that some people just seem to go through life without a care in the world and just achieve whatever they set their mind to? That is something I will address in the following chapters in this book.

What do these really successful people have, that less successful people don't? Belief in themselves and their actions. And that is something I will be addressing as you enter the plethora of information.

In this book, I am going to be giving you valuable strategies that no matter where you are in life, can increase your confidence and success. Now, all of these strategies will be useful however, take the ones you need and discard the rest.

Confidence and self-belief are so important to living a fulfilled, successful life, however, I don't know where you are in life currently. Perhaps you are low in confidence. Maybe you don't like asking questions when you know they should be asked. Potentially, you are doubting your own decisions to the point, you have stopped making them. Or possibly, you don't believe you are good enough for success. If you are here, I am sure that you'll agree with me that this can be very energy sapping and unfulfilling.

So, where do you want to be? Imagine, getting out of bed every morning with a big smile on your face because you feel your confidence oozing through you. Picture a time when no matter what the challenge is, you can make decisions with absolute certainty. Visualise yourself, asking the pertinent questions that no one else in the room is prepared to ask. And envisage having the success you have always dreamed of because you know you have earned it and are worthy of it!

The key here is belief in yourself and your actions with absolute certainty of achievement, also known as confidence.

'Belief in oneself and one's powers or abilities; self-confidence; self-reliance; assurance'
- Dictionary.com

I believe you were born with natural confidence! If you think about it, as a baby you learnt to walk but it is not something you are given, you saw other people doing it and 'believed' you could do it! Eureka!! That is why most people on the planet walk.

We all have the following behaviour pattern:

Thoughts – Beliefs – Decisions – Actions – Results – back to thoughts. It runs in a continuous cycle. You have the choice whether it is a positive or a negative cycle.

For example, when you were learning to walk, you were running this pattern, just like you are now. The difference for so many is that when you were learning to walk, your belief was 'I am going to walk'. No matter how many times you fell, you got up and carried on, creating a positive behaviour pattern and now, I guess you don't even think about walking, you just do it! Why? You have been running that positive pattern for so long now, with so much certainty, that it has become an internalised action. Meaning, you don't think about it as such, you just do it, a bit like breathing.

So, why for many people do they lose their confidence over time?

You will have had experiences throughout life and whilst many of those were fantastic, some of them were painful, emotionally as well as physically.

The world seems more divided than ever, and everywhere I look someone's blaming the government, the economy, and we have governments shouting at one another, wars, it seems like everyone is looking to 'find something wrong' in situations and blame people for their actions. Why? So many people aren't feeling good about themselves and therefore, want to make themselves feel better by taking the spotlight off their lives and blaming others. Instead of taking ownership of their own lives to make it better. Look, there are two ways of looking at things, if you see the tallest office block in front of you, you can either build one that is higher or tear the other one down. Tragically, for most it is the latter action.

For most people, you included no doubt, when you hear something negative said about yourself, you started to believe that it is was true and started to create your behaviours around other people's opinions. Therefore, running that same behaviour pattern, but running it in a negative way that is not empowering you, it is in fact, disempowering you.

Unconsciously, that results in how you view yourself in day-to-day situations. You then created your own 'roadmap' as to how to live your life so you could fit into the world.

This then dictates how you value yourself and the people around you and act accordingly, which determines your confidence in all situations whether they are personal or professional.

This book is designed to help you with strategies to breakthrough your limiting beliefs and be the genuine, authentic, special, unique person you really are and achieve the success you really want and deserve.

TABLE OF CONTENTS

TABLE OF CONTENTS...CONTINUED

A MESSAGE FOR YOU!

Maybe you are like I was, thinking, leave school, get a job and career, find a partner, have 2.4 kids and life would be pretty simple? As if it is on an uphill trajectory and in a straight line.

Then, as you become more experienced in life, you realise, life isn't like a straight line, it is more like a rollercoaster, with peaks and troughs all over the place.

Let me share a bit of my story, let's teleport back to 2015... Life was great, my training business was on course to be the most successful year ever, and my partner had found her real passion and was producing some amazing artwork. We had been planning on working with a couple of art galleries to display her work.

And, if you'd have been with me on the 10th December 2015, you'd have been entering a white, square, clean smelling room that was quite cool and eerie really. Covering about a third of the room was a blue type of shower curtain.

As I pulled back the curtain, there she is. Helen, or Hel as I call her, my partner. Hel is about 5'10", with short brown hair and one of those grey streaks that run from the front to the back of her hair that she absolutely despises. Hel is full of fun, a real joker, the yin to my yang, my rock, my world, my sparring partner, Hel is the love of my life.

"Mr Williams, it is now time for you to leave." It was the voice I didn't want to hear of an officious looking Doctor in a three-quarter length white coat.

You see, we were at the Royal Derby Hospital, here in the UK, and Hel wasn't being prepared for an operation, she was being prepared for the morgue!

I don't know if you have ever experienced something in life where tragedy has happened totally unexpectantly?

For the next couple of months, things weren't too bad under the circumstances, as I was focussing on everyone else. Hel's family and indeed my own, supporting them as anyone would do but the reality was, I was distracting myself by focussing on everyone else. In denial, as I wasn't dealing with the things I needed to deal with in my life, so delaying the inevitable. And, doubting if I was worthy as I couldn't even look after my partner. A bit like putting my head in the sand with everything I needed to deal with, being totally honest.

But I was struggling to get out of bed on a daily basis and if I did, I was watching day-time TV. Well, when I say watching, the reality was, the TV was on, and I was staring at it but not really absorbing what the programme was saying. A bit like a moth in a trance, fixated on a light bulb. When I was talking on the phone to friends and family, putting 'a brave face on' for the call to hopefully hide how I was feeling inside. In essence I was just existing, and the reality was, I was totally 'rock-bottom'. Not only had I lost the love of my life, but I had also basically, lost my business as well as I wasn't even functioning as a human being in my own company.

So, if you would have been with me on this February evening in 2016, you'd have been sat on my corner, black upholstery group, with white walls either side and a red feature wall in front of you. I know the TV is in the right-hand corner and the bookcase is in the left-hand corner of the room but this particular evening, I couldn't see them as the darkness I was feeling inside, was matching the darkness of this non-lit room. I was so depressed, lost, lonely and wondering what is the point of life?

Have you ever felt like that? Totally lost?

I was listening to a lot of music that night which was very melancholic. Songs that resonated with me, that Hel and I used to listen to, or other artists that I felt a real connection with. I just felt that I needed to have a connection to Hel and the better days that we had.

Because I was feeling so down, I hadn't really eaten either that day as I had lost my confidence, and really couldn't see a future for myself as all our plans had totally evaporated like a spell from a Harry Potter movie. In the days leading up I'd had constant thoughts of 'what is the point of going on'?

"I could always jump off the bridge at the bottom of the road, onto the main road, that would be pretty quick, I guess. And you hear of people drinking themselves to death, don't you? The problem is, I'm not keen on alcohol. I guess, it would be easier with a knife then as no-one would find me for a while anyway."

I honestly, don't know what happened next as it is all a blur, it may have been seconds, or even minutes, I have no recollection at all. However, the next thing I knew, I was standing over the kitchen units with a chef's knife across my wrists.

That was scary and my 'lightbulb moment' as I knew I needed to make a decision. Either to stay as I was, just existing rather than living or make the decision to change for the better.

Deep down, I knew I needed help, but I'm a guy and guys don't ask for help do they?

And if I had have done the deed, whatever your beliefs about a greater force, I knew that Hel would have been so ashamed of me.

Now that is a powerful bit of leverage to change!

I went searching for answers to help me and tried a few things, but they didn't help me. So, I started putting some strategies in place and found they started to have an impact for me.

Now, as soon as you decide to change and take action, life becomes a bed of roses, right?

Not necessarily.

On many occasions, I thought I had turned the corner only to find another slide waiting for me to take me back a few steps. It seemed like my life was a piece on one big game of snakes and ladders, and I didn't have control of the dice.

Sound familiar?

But I kept on going as my driver was 'what would Hel think of me' and to make her proud. She had left her impact on the people around her and it was my time to grab hold of that baton and continue with her legacy only in my name now.

So, I had to do much soul searching, and being totally honest, it was very uncomfortable at times, and being brutally transparent, I really struggled.

Visualise this, feeling 'rock bottom', emotionally numb, trying to excavate positive things about myself, my life and what I could do moving forward to get my life back on track to stop existing in order to start living again.

In fact, being honest, I felt I had failed.

But I knew this exercise needed to be done, in fact I decided it wasn't a need, it was something I MUST do. Therefore, I cheated! I put myself into what I imagined were Hel's shoes, and what she would say and do. You see, I was taking the emotional focus off myself, and looking at the situation from a pretend third-party perspective. Imagine, you are watching and enjoying a movie. You are watching that from a third-party perspective where you can see what is going on but cannot interact with it.

Eureka!

It worked for me and suddenly, I could start to see things in a different light and started making notes like crazy whilst I was in that frame of mind. Ok, I ended up scribbling most of them out, but it gave me a starting point. I printed out the summary of my goals and stuck on my fridge so I could see them all the time.

Miraculously, my focus began to change, and I could start to look forwards instead of backwards. Because the way I had been existing was trying to move forward staring in my rear-view mirror and the reality was, I crashed!

Realising I was in such a bad frame of mind before my 'lightbulb moment', I had been talking to myself in such a poor way. It was very self-destructive and again, I hadn't realised it at the time.

Here's the thing, I was using the most negative letter in the alphabet for nearly everything, 'T'. I was telling myself that I can'T do this, and I can'T do that etc.

Perhaps, that is something you can resonate with?

I have since summarised can't as 'Constantly Affirming Negative Talk!' Going through the afore mentioned exercise, I had that epiphany and realised what I had been doing. No wonder I had been struggling!!

It was like trying to move forward wearing concrete slippers, virtually impossible.

Therefore, I dropped the 'T' and started communicating to myself what I COULD do instead of telling myself what I couldn't do, turning can't into CAN!

As I was starting to feel better, I started doing more. Instead of struggling to get out of bed daily, listening to melancholy music, I began to emerge each day with more vigour and listening to more

21

empowering music. For me it was rock music with a good beat, and I also started exercising. It had been a while since I had done any exercise, so my running was really slow and short distances initially. Little by little, this started to improve, just like everything else I had been doing, it was progress over perfection.

There were certain things that I was doing, but in the wrong way so I shifted my thoughts and actions and voila, things started to get better and building some momentum.

I started sharing some of these strategies I had created with other people, and found they were getting great results in a shorter space of time.

By chance, an email crossed my path to become a qualified coach. Hel and I had always been a magnet for others to come to and get their issues resolved, so it seemed a good, logical fit. And, I now had something empowering to focus on, the light at the end of the tunnel.

As I was about to leave for the course in London, I got a massive bout of anxiety and decided to cancel the course. My inner demons were saying *"Dave, how can you become a Master Coach when you can't even master yourself?"*

Maybe you have experienced something similar with your 'inner demons' talking you out of things?

I gave myself a good talking to, being polite there, and rebooked the course as my drive, my MUST, was stronger than my 'inner demons'.

On entering the event room in a hotel by Heathrow Airport, the room was set up like a traditional training room. I sat right at the front, just in front of the stage as I didn't want to miss a thing.

The trainers started their presentations and announced they were Tony Robbins (the world leader in life coaching) trainers. Just then a voice appeared in my head, not my 'inner demons' this time, but my 'inner angel', in fact, it may have even been Hel, I don't know, *"see, you are in the right place."*

So where do you find me now? You find me as an award-winning Results Coach and Speaker who has had the pleasure of speaking in 4 continents around the world. Helping businesses improve their profits and reduce staff turnover, and busy professionals and executives, around the world, overcome their challenges, perform at their peak and start living life again instead of just existing. You see, now that I have had those experiences, I am better equipped to serve myself, and my clients at a greater level and life is great. I can now be more empathetic because of my experiences, although it was very painful at the time.

I now have a wonderful partner, and some very special people in my life who I have had the pleasure of meeting and have enriched my life beyond measure. I am so grateful to everyone who have been a part of my journey and have experienced some amazing things, and met some wonderful people, that I would never have considered possible, many years ago.

The wonderful thing about life now is that I get the privilege of being able to impact people and enhance their lives for the better. Which has resulted in impacting hundreds if not thousands around the world. That is not supposed to sound like hyperbole by any means. Indeed, I am interacting with you right now. You see, it is the ripple effect. Everyone is having an impact on the people they interact with. A bit like dropping a pebble in a pond and watching the ripples expand out from where the pebble was dropped. Here's the thing, those ripples can either be empowering or disempowering. The people I have worked with have turned their ripples into empowering ones, impacting others with their lives.

I can only share this story with you because of making the decision to change. Turning my situation from wanting to change to *"I **MUST** change"*. Having my 'lightbulb moment' was the catalyst as I had to reach my pain threshold before I took that decision. If I hadn't had that moment, and made the right decision, you probably wouldn't be reading this, as no-one will have ever known my story as it would have stopped in 2016.

Has it been a journey with loads of peaks and troughs, "*hell yes*", but it has helped me grow as a person and become a better person for it! In fact, it could be argued that "*I have had more comebacks than Frank Sinatra!*"

Now, obviously I don't know where you are on your journey, but as you have read my story, you will get hit by 'curve balls' along the way. If you are facing challenges currently, then my heart goes out to you but please note, that wherever you are, there is always **"light at the end of the tunnel"**.

Will you make mistakes along the journey, probably, as we are all human and that is how we learn. If you make a mistake, don't worry about it, focus on what you learn from it and make it better the next time.

As Thomas Edison inventor of the light bulb once said, "*I have not failed. I just found 10,000 ways that won't work.*"

Always remember, you are a special, loved, unique individual who has already achieved so many amazing things in life. You have the opportunity to take your life to a better level and have a phenomenal life, impacting others around you. The world needs you, your unique experiences, qualities, and outlook.

Please remember, wherever you are in life, "*it is a chapter in your life and the beauty of it is, 'you are in charge of the quill'. If you don't like it, turn the page, and write another chapter.*" - Dave Williams

So, wherever you are on your journey, the strategies I am about to share with you will help.

STRATEGY NUMBER 1

HONESTY

STRATEGY NUMBER 1
HONESTY

One of the biggest issues I experience when I am working with clients is honesty. I don't mean that in a detrimental way, far from it, I mean being as honest with yourself, as you are with other people.

Always be true to yourself and see things as they really are and not worse than they are!! This can be very challenging for many people as you can be too honest. Let me explain.....

When you are lacking in confidence, you tend to exaggerate situations and make things much worse than they really are.

Take someone who wants to lose weight. I am sure that you know someone who has been in that position, and I certainly do. When they are not losing weight, they tell themselves, and everyone else *"I've tried everything."* Sound familiar? The reality is, they haven't tried everything and are not being honest with themselves. They are telling a story, which is not uncommon, that they have 'tried everything' to pacify their lack of success.

Here's the thing, you, and I, like everyone else gauge reaction from other people in a conscious and other than conscious way. Therefore, when you see a reaction you want, good or bad, you adapt the story in a way to create that reaction again. This is great, if it is a positive reaction, however, it can be detrimental if you do it in a negatively way, so people will give more empathy towards you. Which normally happens with the weight loss example as others tell themselves the same story, so they then get social proof.

Honesty is key to seeing things as they really are.

Being really honest with yourself is often asking yourself difficult question such as: Did I really give everything, and I mean everything, with that particular task, to that relationship?

Being brutally honest, the answer for most people, is probably 'no'. They may well think they did at the time although upon reflection, they realise they didn't.

So why did you not give more? What more could you have done? Don't overthink the answers and go with the first answer you think about, your gut reaction. Acknowledge your answer, learn from it, and move forward.

These can be challenging questions to ask yourself however, it gets to the core of being totally honest with the most important person in your life, you! You see, once you are really honest, and do it consistently, you will not need to think about your answer. Meaning, you will give even more without having to think about it because it becomes the core of you.

Once you do that, you know that you are giving your all. If you are giving your all you know there is nothing 'left in the tank' which breeds confidence as it is always the best of you, and nothing is being kept in reserve!

It helps create clarity about who you are, your values, as your values and integrity are paramount to building your confidence and self-belief.

EXERCISE

Here is the opportunity for you to identify some areas where things could have gone better if you had been a bit more honest with yourself. Honest with your actions, and honest with your core beliefs.

That is not to say this is the opportunity to have regrets and 'beat yourself up', as that is not the purpose of this exercise.

So, grab a piece of paper and write down some of the examples of situations where you could have been more honest with yourself and/or others. Write down your feelings at the time, from what you can remember, and write the alternative actions you could have taken instead, what the potential outcomes would have been and how you would feel if you had taken those actions instead.

"Self – Honesty.
Trying to build confidence whilst lying to yourself is like trying to make friends whilst gossiping behind their backs."

- Dr Friedemann

STRATEGY NUMBER 2

PHYSIOLOGY

STRATEGY NUMBER 2
PHYSIOLOGY

One of the main areas for improving confidence is to get your 'state' right. Meaning, how you are feeling at that time. Everyone feels a little flat at times and that impacts on confidence.

If you think about it, last time you walked down the high street or possibly around your office, you could probably tell people who were in a good mood and those who weren't. It is as if some people are carrying the weight of the whole world on their shoulders. You know, they are walking around with hunched shoulders and frequently with a frown on their face as well.

The key to a great life is to be in a 'peak state', more on this in a couple of strategies. The good news is that you can change your 'state' in a heartbeat!

Here's the thing, for most people, everything is about boxes these days. You get out of a box bed, which is in a box room (square or rectangular bedroom). Go into the kitchen where many people get their breakfast from a cereal box, drive to work in a box called a car, sit in an office box, stare at a computer box all day, drive home in their box car, have a quick meal cooked in a microwave box and watch the tv box in the corner of the room until they go to bed in their box bed of a night.

You, as a human being are not designed to be around straight lines all the time as we all need variety in our lives. It is a bit like being on a hamster wheel that is box shaped, boring and hard to move.

One thing that impacts on your 'state' that most people don't think about is their physiology. In other words, the way you move your body. I like to call it, "your body language with interest." Meaning, the way you move and breathe has an impact on your physiology.

The thing with being in and around boxes most of the time is that you tend to slump after a while with your posture. Therefore, check your posture is correct by having your shoulders back and not slumped over. If you are sitting, stand up and move around, possibly jump up and down a few times as well and do some 'crazy arm movements'. Crazy, meaning you wouldn't do them in your normal position and just have a bit of fun with it. I know, you're probably thinking, "*Dave, are you winding me up here?*" No, I am not and a little secret, I do this all the time and it works!!! When you are in a better 'state', you are more alert and make better decisions. Better decisions lead to better outcomes, which lead to enhanced confidence.

Oh, and don't forget to breathe. Obviously breathing is pretty important in life, but when you are in a poor state you tend to breathe in shallow breaths. When you breathe better, your body utilises oxygen better.

So come on, let's do a breathing exercise together. Make sure your posture is good, either standing straight with your shoulders back or sitting in an upright position.

Now, take a deep breath through your nose and hold it for 3 seconds and then exhale through your mouth. And again, in fact, do those 5 more times and I am sure you will be feeling in a better state.

That alone will help change your state, so you are feeling sharper and more focussed, ready to create better outcomes and feel more confident!

EXERCISE

To get into a great physiological state, move and stand. Put your shoulders back and your hands on your hips and stand like 'Wonder Woman' or 'Superman' and hold that pose for 2 minutes, taking deep breaths in through the nose and out through the mouth. You may feel a little silly initially but who cares right if it helps?

A Harvard University study suggest this reduces the stress hormone Cortisol and increases the Testosterone hormone giving you that boost of certainty and confidence. When I am speaking at events, I often do this exercise with the 'Wonder Woman' and 'Superman' poses. I have done this exercise with Directors, Senior Management and Police Officers of all ranks, and not only does it put a smile on people's faces, but it also helps change their state immediately, and in a good way!

"Expanding your body language through posture, movement and speech – makes you feel more confident and powerful."

- *Amy Cuddy*

STRATEGY NUMBER 3

COMMUNICATION WITH YOURSELF

STRATEGY NUMBER 3
COMMUNICATION WITH YOURSELF

Be honest, do you talk to yourself?

I am sure you do as you need some expert advice now and again, don't you?

However, most people communicate to themselves wrongly!!

Yes, that's right, as when most people talk to themselves, they are doing it in a self-deprecating way. They often ask themselves disempowering questions such as 'Why me?', 'Why am I so stupid?', 'Why does this always happen to me?' etc

The reality is, those types of questions are not going to give you the confidence you need, just erode it. You see, your mind works just like a 'Google search engine'. As the saying goes, "Ask and you shall receive". Human beings don't like unknowns, as their mind requires completion. Have you ever been in a conversation with someone, understood the beginning and the end of the conversation? But you weren't sure what happened in the middle of it so your logical mind, 'made it up' to make it complete. Therefore, if you are asking disempowering questions, you are going to get answers to those questions, that are naturally, disempowering.

Doesn't it make more sense to ask EMPOWERING questions instead? Your 'Google mind' works the same way but will give you quality answers that will give you more belief, certainty, and confidence.

You can either talk yourself into or out of amazing things.

Let me ask you a question? Have you ever gone to make a drink of coffee and found the jar has been moved from where you thought it was located? You are saying to yourself, *"I can't find the coffee, I can't find the coffee, I can't find the coffee, the coffee isn't here."* You eventually call out to the person who you believe moved the jar. *"Where's the coffee?"* To hear a reply, *"It's on the first shelf."* You still can't see it and say to yourself, *"I can't find the coffee, I can't find the coffee, I can't see the coffee."* Then call out, *"the coffee's not here."* Then someone walks in and opens the cupboard, points right at the coffee and says, *"What's that!"* Low and behold, the coffee was in front of you all of the time and you just couldn't see it for looking. You had in fact created a 'blind spot'.

This 'blind spot' is known as a Scotoma. A scotoma is a blind spot or partial loss of vision in what is otherwise a perfectly normal visual field. Using this example, and to explain, what you have done is convince yourself continually by incanting that you cannot see the coffee – *"I can't find the coffee."* So, in essence, you didn't see the coffee initially, and then you affirmed it verbally to yourself loads of times that the coffee wasn't there, therefore, convincing yourself the coffee wasn't there, (more on affirmations/incantations later in the book). When the reality is, the coffee was really there!

That my friend, is how powerful your mind is when it comes to self-communication as it can either help you thrive or help you dive.

If you find yourself asking yourself disempowering questions, stop, thank yourself for asking that question, and ask a more empowering question instead.

It may sound a bit surreal to begin with but with practice, you will find that you rarely ask yourself negative questions anymore.

EXERCISE

Ask yourself better questions and reaffirm yourself, to yourself.

A few examples but obviously, you know the right questions to ask yourself.

When was I successful at this?
If I haven't done this previously, what is something similar I have been successful with?
When did I last achieve this or something similar?
What do I need to do to get better at this?
What can I learn from this?

Using this type of self-questioning gets you to focus on the successes you have had that you can refer to, rather than focussing on things you haven't achieved. So, you are using your 'Google mind' to you advantage. And we all like advantages, right?

"Self-talk is the most powerful form of communication because it either empowers you or defeats you."

- Unknown

STRATEGY NUMBER 4

FOCUS

STRATEGY NUMBER 4
FOCUS

You are probably an expert at this as most people are! Your focus is the key to the quality of your life, as what you focus on, will dictate your thoughts and actions.

Tragically, most people are expert at focussing on the wrong things, problems!

Meaning using your time and effort to focus on your problem, and then just dwell on the problem.

We all have a choice as to what to focus on so wouldn't it make more sense to focus on the solution after identifying the problem? In other words, to focus on where you are going and want, rather what you don't want.

Everybody has problems and every problem has a solution, so it is purely how you approach it.

Now, the wonderful thing is you can change your focus at any time you want to. Let's put it to the test, shall we?

So *do not do what I am about to ask you to do*. To reframe that, *don't do what I am about to instruct you to do*. Are you ready. Ok, here goes, Do NOT THINK about Donald Trump right now!

Be honest, did you think about Mr Trump? Most people tend to, so if you did, you are not alone. What did you think of? It might have been his hair, his posture, his face, anything. You see, that is how easy it is to change your focus as apart from anything else, your mind, like mine, is open to suggestion.

So why do so many people focus on the negative elements to any situation?

I believe that throughout life, you and I are being programmed to focus on the negative – not intentionally, but with so many things seeming negative then it resonates with you are you throughout life.

For example:

You were naturally born with two fears, the fear of falling over and the fear of loud noises. It is your inbuilt survival mechanism which is designed to keep you safe (you may know it as fight or flight mode).

For most people when they are growing up in their very early years, they would have had loads of hugs, kisses and stories being told by their significant family members (mum/dad/aunts and uncles etc).

However, when you started crawling and exploring things, in effect, curiosity took hold like it should do, you no doubt were told off as well, yes?

Now, depending on the situation, if it was deemed that you were putting yourself or others in danger. Your significant family member needed to grab your attention (change your focus) to protect you. Therefore, they probably raised their voice to distract you from what you were doing. Sometimes, even shouting with assertiveness.

Here's the thing, although you had the hugs, kisses etc, this resonated more as it hit your core fear of loud noises – meaning negative.

Then you go to school, how many times did the teacher come into your class and congratulate you all? For most, it didn't happen, but they remember the times when the class was told off, normally in a louder, more assertive voice – negative.

When you are in work, have you ever been called to the boss's office without knowing the reason why? What did you start thinking?

"What have I done wrong? What am I getting a telling off for?" That is what most people's experiences and reactions are, and maybe that resonates with you. See, the negative pattern is already running!

If you watch or listen to the news, how many happy stories do you get? Not many I am sure you will agree.

When I am speaking at events, we normally have some great fun with this section, and it is amazing some of the thoughts that are shared with the 'called to the manager's office' question.

That is why I feel you and I are being programmed to focus on the negative and that in my opinion, is what so many people are experts at focussing on the wrong things, problems.

But, as I have shared previously, you have a choice to focus on something you don't want and disempower you or something that will empower you.

Therefore, choose what you focus on wisely!

You can choose to focus on something funny, a loved one, an outing or holiday you are planning, something you are grateful for, just as easily as focusing on something negative.

EXERCISE

Write down a list of questions you would normally ask yourself in problem situations and then, reframe them into more empowering questions.

Keep these new questions with you either on a piece of paper or a note on your tablet/phone and refer to them when you need to.

The more you use them the more they will become internalised for you making you a problem solver where you have the confidence to deal with anything.

"Focus on the solution or outcome,
not the obstacle or problem."

- *Dean Graziosi*

STRATEGY NUMBER 5

BEING IN A 'PEAK STATE'

STRATEGY NUMBER 5
BEING IN A PEAK STATE

Being in a 'peak state' is so key for life as a whole, especially with your confidence.

But what are the key elements for getting into a peak state? Well, they have covered in the last 3 chapters. They are physiology, communication and finally your focus.

I didn't realise this at the time, but these were the key areas I worked on in my story to get myself back on track.

When I am coaching clients, personal/senior management, or athletes, this is the first thing I work on, changing their 'state'. Most people think that when things aren't going right, you work harder. That is correct in many ways however, you can have the best tools in the world but if your 'state' isn't right, then it can be like trying to achieve the task walking through treacle.

Here's the thing, so many people focus on the strategy to achieve things and the reality is they are wrong. It is 80% mindset and 20% strategy.

Therefore, to increase your confidence, you must improve your state! Now, full disclosure, these terminologies haven't been created by me, they are from the teachings of Tony Robbins, the world's foremost Life Coach. So, I am not trying to take the credit for it at all.

If you are struggling with your confidence, there is one of these elements that are out of kilter: your physiology, your communication, or your focus.

EXERCISE

If you are struggling with your confidence, what needs to change?

Physiology – move your body and make your movements radical from what you were doing. The main thing is to move, change your posture, your breathing, jump up and down whatever you need to do for you to change.

Communication – what questions are you asking yourself? Are they empowering or disempowering questions?

Focus – are you focussing on what you want and the outcome, or what you don't want?

Analyse each one until you identify which one isn't working for you currently and change it.

"That sounds too easy Dave." In essence, it is but if you are new to this, it may take some practice. But once you get used to practicing it, you master it, and it becomes ingrained and automated. Then you have the real secret to upgrading your confidence at any time!

Then just anchor it into your nervous system. Meaning, you will know when you are in peak state as you will feel unstoppable. I have mentioned previously about power poses, and you can create your own 'move' to switch you on into peak state at any time. It could be a 'fist bump', slapping yourself on the chest (not recommended for ladies), whatever works for you, and call out 'YES' at the same time as doing this move as it will enhance the anchoring process for you. Do it several times until you know that it will take you to a peak state anytime you want to!

"A poor state is like a flat tyre. You need to change it to get to your destination"

- Dave Williams

STRATEGY NUMBER 6

CHANGE YOUR STORY

STRATEGY NUMBER 6
CHANGE YOUR STORY

You, like everyone else, have your own story, of what has happened in your life to get where you are in life right now.

For some, they have been wonderful stories and for many, they have been, shall we say, challenging. Obviously, I have no idea regarding your story but are you using your story to your advantage, or letting it hold you back?

Whatever your story is, you can use it as a millstone or a milestone. Meaning, you can use your story as a weight around your neck or, as a journey of inspiration.

Let me tell share a story with you: There were two twin boys who grew up experiencing absolutely everything together. They had an interesting childhood as they had a physically abusive father who was also a drunk. As the boys matured, they went their separate ways in life and a local news station heard of their story and went in search of the two men to discover their stories. Upon finding the first brother, the news station went to interview him. He was down on his luck, living on the streets, and on handouts. When the reporter heard his story she asked, *"so how did you end up here?"*. To which he replied, *"with a father like mine, how could I have been anything else?"* The reporter then found the second twin to interview. He was a successful CEO of a multimillion-dollar international organisation. When the reporter heard his story she asked, *"so how did you end up here?"* To which he replied, *"with a father like mine, how could I have been anything else?"*

It is fair to say, with this story, both men had the same upbringing but obviously a totally different outcome. Why, because one viewed his story as a millstone and the other viewed his story as a milestone.

Whilst this story is a fictional story to my knowledge, a metaphor if you will, I am sure that you know of many people who have had a challenging story in their lives but have used that as a turbo charge to maximise their life.

When I work with personal clients, I hear all sorts of stories as I am sure you can imagine, and I am always in awe. Indeed, some of their stories are so exceptional and inspiring to me, I use them as a driver for me in my life.

Now, for obvious reasons, I am not going to share their stories as that is privileged information, but if you want some stories of inspiration then look at Oprah Winfrey, J.K. Rowling, Eddie Jaku, or a dear friend of mine, Kerrie Atherton (Stories of Hope - Australia), to name some. Their stories are truly inspirational and show how someone can turn their potential millstones (stories) to milestones.

Thank and congratulate yourself for getting to this point in life, as without your experiences, you would not be where you are now. Then it is time to decide what you need to make your life even better. Write them out on a piece of paper and just brainstorm them. Then decide on a plan of your greatest priorities and find someone to help you if you can't do it on your own.

So, no matter your story, you can use it as you see fit, as a millstone to deprive you of your confidence or as a 'turbo charged rocket' for your confidence, and your future.

Always remember, *"Your past is just your apprenticeship for your future"*- Dave Williams.

EXERCISE

Grab a piece of paper and a pen for this exercise and draw a line down the centre of the page.

Let's take your old story and write on the left-hand side of the page. Now 'flip it' to create a new more empowering, one. Ask yourself the following questions, then write your new story on the right-hand side of that piece of paper.

What is something good that came out of your story?
What do you think was an obstacle in your life, but created the skills that made you what you are today?
What unique capabilities do you now have?
Find the good that can come from your story as there is a better story for you. What is it?

Focus on the good things, the empowering things you have now thought of and utilise them for your future.

"Owning our story can be hard but not nearly as difficult as spending our lives running away from it."

- Brené Brown

STRATEGY NUMBER 7

BUILD YOUR FOUNDATIONS STRONG!

STRATEGY NUMBER 7
BUILD YOUR FOUNDATIONS STRONG

Have you ever been in a situation where suddenly you have 'blown up' at your partner because they haven't done a simple task, like take the bins out for example?

Yes? Well, a little secret, most people have. The reality is, it is not the fact that they didn't do that task, it is all the other things they have or haven't done, that you thought they could have done or done better. It then all comes 'to a head' and that is when the 'blow up' happens. It's known as 'stacking'!

Here's the thing, you do that to yourself as well. Unfortunately, with all the negative things that you feel you have not been good at, made mistakes with, feel embarrassed, felt like you failed etc. When you do this though, you are building your foundations poorly.

I'm sure you'll agree, that is like building your confidence foundations on sand. It isn't going to last!

So, wouldn't it make sense to build your foundations strong and stack in a more constructive, empowering way? Giving you 'the edge' over most people on the planet! Therefore, identify these areas where you could have done better, and acknowledge them, knowing you can improve. Don't dwell on them just be aware of your previous actions and your attached emotion as this was learning and experience.

Then, with the exercises, you will be completing an exercise in 'power stacking'. This way you will building your foundations strong and enhancing your confidence.

EXERCISE

The first part of your exercise is to grab a pen and paper and go through a brainstorming session. Now before you do this, get into a 'peak state' as covered in Strategy number 5, as it will be more impactful for you! List down all the things you have been successful at. Don't just think of all the big things you have achieved, think of the smaller ones as well and just write them down. Going to school for the first time, going out on a date with someone for the first time, learning to drive (if applicable), starting a new job, getting out of bed every day etc.

When you have one listed also ask yourself 'and what else was there?' (Most people just look at the surface subject but, in most cases, there was more than one thing actioned/achieved). List them all and then put them in some sort of order and have them so you can see them all the time. When you go through each one, take yourself back to that time, see what you saw, hear what you heard and feel what you felt and fell that pride in achieving those tasks.

The second part is to create a journal and note down daily (I strongly suggest daily) or weekly, all the 'wins' you have achieved. All the things you have accomplished that were successful and the things you overcame. Refer to this journal frequently and remind yourself of your 'wins'.

That way you are keeping your positive stacking topped up and it will help internalise your confidence thinking so it becomes part of you, consistently!

"Knowledge is a compounding investment.
you draw on it again and again."

- Jenna Koucher

STRATEGY NUMBER 8

KNOW YOUR WHY!

STRATEGY NUMBER 8
KNOW YOUR WHY!

Knowing your Why meaning, the reason for doing something, is such an important element with everything you do, alas so many people don't even think of why they are doing something or want something.

Without having a clear outcome, you will not invest all of yourself into the outcome and when you don't achieve the result you want, will 'stack it' in the negative pile of 'never achieving'. The reality is that you didn't have the 'buy in' in the first place and therefore, you were setting yourself up to fail before you even started.

When I coach clients, one of the first things I ask is *"what do you want?"*
Quite often, silence...............................
If I then ask, *"what don't you want"*, then it is a different story and I get lists of things people don't want. Not ideal, but at least it is a start as we can always 'flip it'.

Why is that the 'what you don't wants' come so freely? As I have mentioned previously, I believe we are programmed to focus on the negative.

Here's the thing, when you know what you want to achieve, you are on the right path. When you know your why, and you attach an emotion to it – wham, that is when you are igniting your inner turbo driver. That alone give you more certainty which will breed more confidence.

When you are certain of your outcome, you will get challenges along the way as that is normal however, this is where the beauty of knowing your outcome comes to the fore. When you have also attached a strong enough emotional 'why' to it, you will then become unstoppable. 'Whatever it takes', right?

I have mentioned previously that your mind works like a Google search engine. When you get challenges, as yourself more empowering questions as to how to overcome these challenges and you will get the answers you need, and additional opportunities will arise.

Please note, your mind is such a phenomenal tool and when you know your why/outcome/destination, it works like a guidance system on a rocket. The rocket knows what its destination is and because of changes in the atmosphere etc, it gets blown off course but because it knows its destination, it realigns to reach its goal.

That is how your mind works as well! Pretty cool eh?

Also, when you know your outcome, you will notice things around you that will help you achieve that goal. These things have always been there however, you just haven't been focussing on them.

Have you ever had a new car and as you drive off for the first time and you are driving home, you notice a similar car, driving in the opposite direction? And then another, and possibly another one as well. You then may start thinking, I didn't realise this type of car was so popular?

What is the difference? Suddenly, have all these cars just materialised as they know you have just purchased a new car? No, your mind is just open to accepting these images whereas, previously it wasn't.

That, combined with knowing your outcome, being 'in state', having your own emotional attachment to the outcome, communicating to yourself in the right way, will drive you to achieve amazing things as you believe you WILL achieve it and that alone will drive your confidence.

When your 'why' is that strong, you will take the uncomfortable action you need to take, one step at a time, and with each step, your confidence will grow.

EXERCISE

Grab a pen and piece of paper and draw a line down the middle of the page.

On the left-hand side, write down the goal you want to achieve.

On the right-hand side, write down your 'why' you want to achieve it. Once you have written your 'why', now attach an emotion or emotions to why you want it.

You see, most people when they write their 'why', they put a superficial answer such as 'I need it'. When you attach a real emotion, or several real emotions to it, it becomes so much more powerful and when it is that powerful - you will become unstoppable, and your confidence will just grow with every step and action!

"Find your why and you'll find your way."

- John C Maxwell

STRATEGY NUMBER 9

GRATITUDE

STRATEGY NUMBER 9
GRATITUDE

What is Gratitude? It comes from the latin word 'Gratus' and means pleasing, thankful.

I feel the term Gratitude is often overused and when it is used, quite often without any real meaning and emotion behind it.

Have you ever been out with friends, and it's been a rough night? Then you find yourself saying at the end of the evening 'thanks it's been lovely'. I'm sure you have! If we are being honest with ourselves, we've ALL done it at some stage of our lives.

See, for real gratitude, I don't mean it is a superficial way, you need to mean it from your heart! With honesty, sincerity, and love.

Because when you do anything with love, it's always honest and improves your state. And as I have mentioned previously, being in a great state is so important.

So, let me ask you a question, what are you grateful for?

"Well, I don't feel grateful about anything in my life currently Dave!" You may well be thinking? If you are, then a reframe of the question might be, *"So what COULD you feel grateful for?"*

You see, most people just think of their life 'in the now' which is great, however, then take a 'snapshot' of things at that time. If you are going through a challenging time, don't focus on what you haven't got, covered in Strategy Number 6, your story. Instead of looking at the bigger picture of your life and focus on the things you have got. Meaning, who or what could you feel grateful for having/being in your life/who's had a positive impact on your life? There are so many things around us that we all just take for granted. I have certainly been guilty of this in my life.

One thing that I am grateful for every day is that I wake up and get out of bed! There are so many people that would love to be able to do that, who can't.

A personal client of mine recently moved house and has done really well for herself. Starting off life in a council estate, grafting with absolute commitment and dedication and now lives in a beautiful house in the country. Why am I sharing this? Because she is so grateful to be able to look out of the window and see wildlife every day. The birds, rabbits and be able to see trees as she didn't notice these things previously. She can just look out of the window and have gratitude immediately because of her journey to get her there!

So can you with elements of your life. You may not be able to look out of the window and see such wildlife, but you will have opportunities, people, experiences, you can be grateful for.

A quick 'hack' that I use on a regular basis is think of 5 things or people I am grateful for. I then use one hand and as I touch my thumb to each finger, I call out what I am grateful for. Immediately it changes my state and I focus on those people or situations. I do that even when I am in an excellent state as it reignites me even more. That is something you can do whenever you want to.

The reason is, when you are grateful, it improves your state which then impacts and improves your confidence.

EXERCISE

What 5 things can you bring to your mind and be grateful for right now?

Do this for 10 days and before you know it, 50 things of gratitude that you can call on at any time!

"It is not happiness that brings us gratitude, it is gratitude that brings us happiness."

- *Anonymous*

STRATEGY NUMBER 10

LIVE IN THE NOW!

STRATEGY NUMBER 10
LIVE IN THE NOW!

This may seem a bit of a surreal strategy, however, for many, it will be the most enlightening.

I'm going to ask you to use your imagination. *"What are you doing Dave, more work?"* Yes, and as ever, there is a reason.

Now, imagine you have 3 buckets in front of you, you can choose the colours of them if you wish, I normally go with red on the right, yellow in the middle and green on the left-hand side. The red one is your past and it is full to the brim of water (your memories, references, and experiences). The yellow one has some water in it as that is what you are experiencing now, reading this book for example, and the green, your future, is totally empty.

Here's the thing, so many people grab a sponge and try to bail the red bucket into the yellow bucket and carry all their past experiences into 'the now'. The drawback with that is you will never learn and experience new things because the yellow 'now' bucket is full of your past, so you have no room to put new experiences into it. Therefore, in essence, you are stagnating. This is one of the biggest challenges my clients have before they start working with me. Focussing on their red bucket all the time, instead of focussing on creating the foundations for their green bucket.

Why? Society is not exactly encouraging success. So many negative stories are being focussed on and repeated either in conversations and/or the written word. It is as if you and everyone else is being placed in a trance of what to focus on, think and believe. Not what is right for you to enhance your life.

Stop living in the past as *"the past is a place of reference and not a place of residence"* - unknown.

It is a bit like driving using only the rear-view mirror to move forward. If you do that all the time, guess what? You're going to crash!

Living in the past will potentially crucify your confidence instead of living in 'the now' and creating your future. The reality is life is all about new experiences and growing.

Yes, you have the red bucket to refer to but always remember to ring out your sponge as you need to take new learnings with you when you create your future in the green bucket. What you invest in now, you and your current actions, will create your future. Therefore, doesn't it make sense to give yourself the best start possible?

Invest in yourself and your actions now, to create the next compelling chapters in your life with love, wonder and excitement. Let go of what has happened and focus on having the compelling future you always dreamed of.

Draw the proverbial line in the sand, be thankful for all your previous experiences and use them and enhance them with new confident experiences. When you look back 12 months, 5 years, 10 years from now and look at where you are and where you have come from, you will thank yourself for the decisions you make today.

EXERCISE

Grab a piece of paper and draw a line down the middle of the page.

On the left-hand side, write down the experience that has been holding you back and sapping your confidence.

Now, on the right-hand side, write down why you are going to let it go and how it is going to propel you for greater things.

"Your past is your apprenticeship
for the future."

- Dave Williams

STRATEGY NUMBER 11

LISTEN TO THE RIGHT PEOPLE

STRATEGY NUMBER 11
LISTEN TO THE RIGHT PEOPLE

Maybe you are like me and have some amazing people in your life?

And, have you noticed that most of them have their own opinions? Let's be honest, we all have our own opinions, don't we?

Here's the thing, most opinions aren't based on any facts, they are based on references. Meaning, personal experiences, other people's experiences, things that have been heard and seen, or even things that have just been made up.

The drawback is, there is so much information out there these days that it can be difficult to ascertain what is fact and what is fiction, or just opinion.

Have you got anyone in your life that just wants to share their opinion of what you are and have been doing? Let's be honest, most of us have.

The reality is, when the important people in your life share their 'golden nuggets' of information, it is from their perspective, and they are not living your life. Most of the time, they are doing it through love, and want to do their utmost to care, protect, and keep you safe. So not meant in a negative way.

However, their values aren't necessarily the same values as yours and whilst they are doing it with the best of intentions, this will quite often impact your confidence.

Because they are your best friend, you don't need to take their advice. So many people go to their best friend for relationship advice for example, and this friend, however well intended, hasn't managed to keep a relationship in the last 20 years, isn't going to be the right person for you if you want relationship advice!

A dear family member of mine is a classic example. Don't get me wrong, I love her to bits but, and it is a big but, she has a wonderfully unique knack of turning every positive into a negative! I know, really inspiring, eh? I know she is doing it out of love for me and wanting to keep me safe, however, my outlook on life and experiences are different to hers.

Maybe you can resonate with that, about someone in your life?

Naturally, I don't go to this family member for advice with certain parts of my life, I go to people who have experienced life in a way that can help me, not restrict me.

The same applies to you, go to people who will inspire and fill your cup up. The ones who have been where you are now and have the lived experiences to advise and inspire you. Immediately, that will give you more confidence as you will have a mentor who has had similar experiences to you, will know many of the pitfalls and know how to overcome them.

EXERCISE

Write a list of people you know who are trustworthy and will be honest with you.

Then put a note next to their names of the experiences you know they have overcome, and they will then be a good resource for you should you need one.

Alternatively, find someone not in your current network than can help you with experience in what you are looking to overcome.

That will help you reduce decades into days to propel you forward, inspiring you and helping increase your confidence at the same time.

"The best people to listen to are those who have already been successful accomplishing exactly what you are looking to accomplish."

– Brian Koslow

STRATEGY NUMBER 12

'NEWS DIET'

STRATEGY NUMBER 12
'NEWS DIET'

Do you ever watch, listen to, or read the news? If yes, how many happy stories do you see/hear? Not many I bet. Maybe you even feel a bit flat after watching or listening to the news?

Let me as you a question, is it possible for two people to experience the same things and view them differently? Of course, it is, and the reason is the emotional attachment they each attach to their experiences. One may well choose to feel good about an experience, and the other feel bad about the same experiences.

I will let you into a secret, the age-old adage of "bad news sells because the amygdala is always looking for something to fear" - Peter Diamandis, is so true. Your basic brain function, the amygdala part of your brain, is designed to keep you safe. You may well know it as your lizard brain or pre-historic brain associated with 'fight or flight'. It helps coordinate responses to things in your environment, especially those that trigger an emotional response. This structure plays an important role in fear and anger.

What you need to realise is that news channels are not a just a service anymore, they are a business. They will obviously sell themselves as a service, and the reality is, they are serving themselves. It is all about ratings and the higher they are in the ratings, the more 'customers' they have to sell to. It maybe commercials so they can increase their own revenue or maybe even sell their own programmes.

They know how to activate your amygdala part of the brain because if it's bad news, you'll carry it with you and if it is good news, you don't normally pay attention. There is so much news available now with the mainstream channels but also social media, hence, more competition Therefore, they 'sensationalise' the headlines to grab your attention because they need to capture your focus, so they can share their stories

Here's the thing, Fear sells! They are doing what they feel is right for their business. Not necessarily you or I, the consumer.

And the reality is, you are being bombarded with, and programmed by these negative stories all the time. Your fearful emotions are being triggered, unintentionally by yourself, it is bound to have an impact on your state and ultimately, your confidence.

If you keep on bombarding your brain with negative 'communication' you will begin to believe it and it will impact on the way you think, move, and behave.

Therefore, start a 'news diet' and focus on what you need to do, and fill yourself with great, empowering stories instead. You may be thinking, *"well Dave, I need to know what is going on in the world."* That is a very fair comment if you are. Here's the thing, most people in your life will be watching the news and anything pertinent, you will get to hear it from others. So, you will not really be missing out.

Learn about people who have been successful in their lives. Possibly who have risen from adversity and are now living a life of fulfilment. That will be so much more powerful for you and fill you with possibilities and wonder, rather than fear and dread.

Feed your mind with information that will aid you and not destroy you. Your mind is like a computer as I have mentioned, and you can only get out of it what you put in it. When you do this, it will trigger great emotions, change your state to a better/great level and it is so much easier to feel confident in yourself and your surroundings.

EXERCISE

A nice easy exercise for this strategy and no pen or paper required.

Stay away from watching and listening to the news for a week/month and see how you feel.

"There is just news.
there is no good or bad, just news."

- *Master Oogway*

STRATEGY NUMBER 13

PROXIMITY

STRATEGY NUMBER 13
PROXIMITY

It can be a challenge sometimes when you are feeling 'on top of the world' and the people around you are all airing their opinions at the negative elements of society and life as a whole. Indeed, some of these people can be people who you love dearly, however, their outlook on life is different to yours.

If you find yourself in that situation, maybe ask this question in your mind 'with that attitude, I wonder what they are challenged by at the moment?'

The reality is, these people are not helping you with your confidence levels and like most human beings, it can be a massive drain on your confidence and self-worth. You have the choice to ignore what is being said, listen to it but don't digest it. Meaning, let what is being said 'go in one ear and out of the other' or take it to heart and add your emotional attachment to it.

The easiest thing is to change your proximity to people who are forward thinking, and outcome orientated. Feed your mind with captivating conversations that can stretch you, inspire you, motivate and compliment you. This can be done either physically or via audio/video.

Changing your proximity to open minded people can help massively as it removes any 'blinkers' you may have on and can really open your eyes to reality, and not just a small percentage of other peoples limited beliefs. This alone will be a massive confidence boost and anchor those new feelings with taking additional action.

If your current circle of people aren't serving you in life, let them go as you have outgrown them and find better people.

EXERCISE

Find yourself an autobiography of someone you admire (book or audio) and absorb the information. You see, most successful people have had, and sometimes do still have, issues with their confidence at times.

Then find another.

Immersion in these types of information can be spellbinding and help anchor your confidence beliefs as they have lived it as well.

"Choose to be in close proximity to people
who are empowering...
who see the greatness in you."

- Wayne Dyer

STRATEGY NUMBER 14

IMPOSTER SYNDROME

STRATEGY NUMBER 14
IMPOSTER SYNDROME

Imposter Syndrome as it is now frequently called, is where an individual doubts their skills, talents and accomplishments and have an internalised fear of being a fraud. Maybe that is something you can relate to?

There are many people I have had the pleasure of meeting in all walks of life in very senior levels and many of them either do or have had to deal with imposter syndrome, even Directors and Business owners of multi £m companies.

So, if you feel that way, you are not alone.

This is a quite frequent feeling with my personal clients and the thing with imposter syndrome, your mind is working overtime and creating its own little story around why you aren't good enough. You need to look at things as they are and not what you perceive them to be. As I have referred to with previous strategies.

Meaning, your mind, like everyone else's, expands on things that aren't real and then it tries to justify those thoughts. If it cannot find something credible, it will create something for you.

It is time to retire the 'storyteller' and listen to the truth that you also know. But maybe you were told when you were younger 'don't get too big for your boots' or something similar. That maybe practical for when you were younger but not now.

Again, referring to what has been mentioned with previous strategies, especially 'building your foundations strong,' you will have had experiences in life, and it is the meaning you give to them.

Maybe, when you were about 3 years old, you had some family members who called around to your house and you were shy. Resonate?

Perhaps, when you were about 10 you did something, and you were told it was stupid. Resonate?

Maybe, when you were about 15 you did something that made you embarrassed, asked someone on a date or were asked on a date. Resonate?

If any or all of the 3 previous questions did resonate with you, it is because it applies to the vast majority of people although obviously the ages may differ.

Alternatively, I am sure that when you were 3 you did something bold that should resonate.

Likewise, when you were about 10, you did something extra ordinary and brave, that should resonate.

Maybe when you were about 15, you also did something that was empowering, unexpected and you achieved something you really wanted. This again should also resonate.

Now is the time to realise your true self and recognise your real achievements. As YOU have done them and no-one else.

You are not an imposter at all as you have achieved great things in your life. So, instead of looking at yourself as an imposter, think of yourself as an expert who can share those experiences with others who need that guidance.

Yes, this is a very similar exercise to Strategy 7 however, it has a different slant and will be enforcing the previous exercise as well.

EXERCISE

Grab a piece of paper, journal or open a new page on your tablet/laptop and title it 'Things I have done Successfully' and start writing them down one by one. You can just use a sentence or write a little paragraph about them if you want. It doesn't matter how 'big' the task was, just write it down quickly and don't over think them. And keep adding to them over time.

Now, take a step back and read them all. As you are reading them, feel what you felt at the time of accomplishing those tasks and let that pride and energy, especially if it was a big thing, and let that pride ooze throughout your body and feel your confidence grow, increasing your certainty that you can adapt and deal with anything, every time.

"I have written eleven books, but each time I think 'uh oh, they're going to find me out now.'"

- *Maya Angelou*

STRATEGY
NUMBER 15

PROCRASTINATION

STRATEGY NUMBER 15
PROCRASTINATION

Procrastination is the action of delaying or postponing something. The word has origin from the Latin 'procrastinatus', which itself evolved from the prefix pro-, meaning "forward," and crastinus, meaning "of tomorrow." - Wikipedia. I think that sums it up so well.

So, do you struggle with procrastination? Most people do at times but what are the reasons why you procrastinate? By the way, there is a difference between procrastinating and being a procrastinator.

A procrastinator habitually puts things off all the time whilst procrastinating is normally putting things/tasks off occasionally. There is a difference. So why do you put things off?

Several reasons to putting things off, as you may be waiting for additional information to be able to complete the task and that is a genuine action however, the main issue is when you know you need to do something but you 'put the brakes on' and don't follow through.

Why?

Most people don't take the action they know they should be taking because of a lack of confidence in their abilities in achieving the desired result. Therefore, the fear of judgement rears its head as 'it won't be perfect' and MOST people have been there at one stage or another. Please remember, no-one is perfect and just do the best you can.

If you have several things to do then start with the most difficult task first, get the result and get it out of the way. Next!

Every time you take action instead of procrastinating, you are reaffirming to yourself that you are a doer and that alone will help increase your confidence because you are taking control by taking action.

EXERCISE

When you feel you are procrastinating, use the 5 second rule as created by Mel Robbins in her bestselling book 'the 5 second rule'.

You know the task that needs completing, you can start to overthink the situation and maybe talk yourself out of taking action.

Instead, decide on your action and instead of overthinking the situation, as Mel's book suggests, count yourself down, 5, 4, 3, 2, 1, GO!, and take ACTION.

"You don't have to see the whole staircase, just take the first step."

- Martin Luthor King, Jnr

STRATEGY NUMBER 16

IMPACT OTHERS

STRATEGY NUMBER 16
IMPACT OTHERS

So far, I have been purely focussed on you and giving strategies to internally help with your confidence, I am going to change that for this strategy, and get you to focus externally, on other people.

"What, how is that going to help me?" I hear you cry.

Have you ever been in a situation, and someone has said something nice to you, possibly given you a compliment when you weren't expecting it? If you have, how did that make you feel? I bet it changed your mood and probably felt appreciated and possibly important.

When was the last time you are in a shop buying something, and ask the assistant how they were and how their day was going? Even better, if you saw their name badge on their clothing used their name as it personalises the question. Do you think that they may have got the same feelings you had in the previous example? Simple, isn't it? Of course, it is!

Why?

You will notice a positive change in their state because someone, you, have taken an interest in them as a person and not just someone there to do a job. It may be a verbal *"thank you"* or a bigger smile than before you asked the question. The thing is you are having a positive impact on their life and if you appreciate that is happening, it'll have a positive effect on you also.

This in turn will help you improve your state and with doing that impact your confidence as well.

I cannot tell you how often I have personally done this and had people find me later on in the day or week, assuming our paths have crossed again, and thanked me for taking an interest in them. Some because they were feeling 'down' that day and just going through the motions, others because they felt like someone cared.

People like to be noticed and acknowledged; I am sure that you do. So, give that feeling to others and reap the benefits yourself as well. It is the classic example of 'paying it forward'. Give first and you shall receive although maybe not immediately, but, as time moves on. It has happened since time and immemorial.

Why?

Because it works! People will remember your actions and how it made them feel. But deep down, it will also make you feel good and the better you feel, the more confident you will feel because it changes your state and physiology.

Also, because you have made that person feel better, they will normally do something similar to someone else. So, your simple action has then started a ripple effect of impacting several people with that simple action - powerful!! If you think about it, in essence, that is what Greta Thunberg did. She started with the school pupils and before too long, she has created a movement even speaking in front of world leaders. It all starts with the first one.

The key to life is giving!

Is everyone going to reciprocate? No, because many people don't have the same outlook as you and that is down to them. If you have given, it means you are acting from the heart and giving with absolute congruency which alone, will improve your confidence.

EXERCISE

Consciously think about who's life you can impact each day, whether it be in person or via a call/message/email.

Just give them a call or send them a message, even if you haven't been in touch with them for a while and let them know you still value them.

Start your conversation with *"how are you today"* or *"what is great about your life today"*, whatever you feel is right.

"In a gentle way, you can shake the world."

- Mohandas 'Mahatma' Ghandi

STRATEGY
NUMBER 17

FEEDBACK

STRATEGY NUMBER 17
FEEDBACK

Don't you just love feedback?

You are probably reading this and thinking *"yes when it is good feedback".*

Hey, don't we all love great feedback? The reality is it isn't going to be great and what we want to hear all of the time.

Many people go into a place of fear when they hear the term feedback as they are in a poor state and they automatically think of the worst scenario. Maybe you have experienced that? It can quite often be compounded by those two interesting words, 'constructive feedback'. It is a marketing term where they are looking to take away the shock value of negative feedback.

It is all B/S!

This is about YOUR confidence so look at it for what it is in reality, and don't start your mind creating all sorts of stories and imagining all sorts of stories, as you can end up 'destroying yourself' mentally.

I normally share this at speaking engagements, look at feedback for what it really is, either:

WINNING or LEARNING

I am sure that you have heard the story about Colonel Sanders and Kentucky Fried Chicken (KFC). At the age of 65 years, and with a Social Security check for $105 a month, he went about trying to franchise his chicken recipe. Wearing his famous white suit and living in his car most of the time, he went about knocking on doors of restaurants, selling his recipe. You may well know KFC as a household name, but he received feedback along the way, from 1009 restaurateurs telling him 'No'.

It was only his determination and belief that kept him going and on his 1010 restaurant, he received his first 'yes', and the rest is history.

Obviously, he treated his feedback as learning, and how to do things differently for success. He didn't start creating all sorts of stories and continually had the belief and confidence that someday, he would win.

Here's the thing, treating feedback for what it actually is, is key. Either things have gone really well or, there is some work to be done. Maybe it is application, skills to be learnt, better communication between parties (more often than not, this is a key issue). Whatever it is though, be real about the situation.

When it is a 'win' stack it in your positive stacking and when it is a 'learning', what needs to happen to make it/you better next time?

Possibly, who do you need to become to be better next time? Be realistic though and don't dwell on it but take action. We all have 'off days' for whatever reason. Sometimes we know the reason and sometimes we cannot pinpoint the real reason.

If it happens, put it down to experience and learn from it and accept feedback comes from other people's opinions.

Feedback, when treated the correct way is a confidence enhancer. Either it is great, and you are along the right path, or it is great because you have identified an area of improvement. You see, it is win/win, provided you treat it the right way.

When it is a win/win scenario, you know you are winning so let it boost your confidence and you know you cannot lose.

EXERCISE

Grab a pen and paper and write down some of the times you have received negative feedback.

Now, write underneath what the good news that came out of the situation. In other words what was the learning – additional skills required, a different approach was required etc.

Also make a note of the times you have received great feedback as well.

Again, you are using these positive feedback situations to stack in the right way, impacting your confidence.

"It takes humility to seek feedback. it takes wisdom to understand it, analyse it and appropriately act upon it."

- Stephen Covey

STRATEGY NUMBER 18

MISTAKES

STRATEGY NUMBER 18
MISTAKES

Raise your hand if you've ever made a mistake.

Excellent!!!! It shows you're human, being honest, and alive!!!!!

We all make mistakes as we are human beings and that is how we learn, well hopefully anyway :)

Let's look at the word mistake - 'An act or judgement that is misguided' - Definitions from Oxford Languages. So, it is a misguided act or judgement, so not intentional and more often than not, it is down to a lack of understanding in the subject/person.

One of the main reasons you don't want to make a mistake is it triggers a fear inside of you, which everyone has. The fear of 'I'm not good enough (make a mistake)', 'I'll be judged' and break that down further, 'I'll never be loved'. Being loved is one of the core needs of a human being and it is just your defence mechanism 'kicking in' to protect you.

Maybe you have heard of the 'flight, fight or freeze' scenario with our bodies. It is a message just telling you to be prepared as you may need to take action, because of a fear. It is your minds default setting if you will, to keep you safe. That is why you will feel bad if you have made a mistake.

The challenge we all have currently is that society seem to be focussing on everything negative, and everyone seems to be looking for others to make mistakes.

However, you are where you are today because you HAVE made mistakes and as I say, the key is to learn from them to increase your skills and improve.

When you have made a mistake, accept it for what it is and don't make the issue bigger than it actually is. Ask yourself 'what is the learning here, so I can do it better next time?' Then act upon it. Unless you have a time machine, you cannot change it just what you can do in the future. To reframe that, just 'let it go' as you have made the decision what to do in the future if the situation arises again.

I am sure you know of Richard Branson and his Virgin empire. But do you remember Virgin Cola, Virgin Brides or Virgin cars? The likelihood is no. He's made many mistakes and states: 'Over the years, my team and I have not let mistakes, failures or mishaps get us down.' And I think it is fair to say he knows a thing or two about success, don't you?

Have you ever used Bubble Wrap? Maybe you are like I am and find it irresistible not to burst the pockets of air when you see some. But did you realise, Bubble Wrap is actually a failure?

Interestingly, engineers Marc Chavannes and Al Fielding created bubble wrap in 1960 in an attempt to create a trendy new textured wallpaper. This was a total failure, as was a later attempt to market it as housing insulation. When the wrap was eventually used by IBM to package a newly launched computer during transport, it suddenly became an overnight success. Today, few people even realise that bubble wrap began as an abject failure.
- Source: Forbes magazine

Sometimes, when you feel like you have failed, because you have made a mistake, you are just preparing for something greater than you can see right now. When I am speaking at an event, I tell the audience to make mistakes. Now obviously, I don't mean purposefully, I mean as long as they are genuine and don't cost millions of pounds, as that is how you learn.

As I mentioned with the previous strategy, it is feedback and know you are another step closer to your success. That alone will be a confidence booster to you.

EXERCISE

On a piece of paper put a line down the middle of the page from the top to the bottom.

On the left-hand side of that line, list down 5 mistakes you feel you've made. On the right-hand side of the page write what the learning is and how you can do better next time.

Then just take a mental note of it and if the situation arises again, you will know what to do better.

"I've never made a mistake. I've only learned from my experience."

- Thomas A Eddison

STRATEGY NUMBER 19

REJECTION

STRATEGY NUMBER 19
REJECTION

A big subject for many people as everyone will feel rejected at times. No-one likes to feel rejected because, everyone wants and needs, to feel wanted and loved.

Maybe you are like the majority of people and if you feel you have been rejected, you personalise it and make it about something you have said/done or something you should have said or done. Perhaps, you are also like most people and then overthink the situation and make it all about you, your actions, even when it is not your fault?

So, if someone you love said to you 'I love you', you would personalise that as well. If the person who said it meant that much to you, you would feel loved, possibly, warm and fuzzy inside as well. If your neighbour/best friend said 'I love you' instead of the love of your life, it would feel different right?

You see, it is the meaning that you give it that gives it it's power and you can choose whether it is going to be an empowering meaning or a disempowering meaning.

The reality is, in most cases, rejection is a breakdown in communication. Confident people treat rejection as it really is, the timing just wasn't right at that particular time, possibly a misunderstanding, and someone has then reacted differently to what you imagined would happen. They don't dwell on it.

I am sure you have heard of Disney World and maybe you have been. The reality is, if Walt Disney had taken rejection personally, the magical experience for so many would never have been created. Walt was rejected by 302 banks before finding one that was willing to finance his dream. You see, he didn't take it personally he just realised the timing with the 302 banks wasn't right. He didn't let it hold him back or influence his actions.

Maybe you have applied for jobs before now and not been successful. It has happened to virtually everyone. I am sure there would have been disappointment, but you wouldn't have dwelt on it for ages.

Rejection, or improper timing, is something that happens in life and there is no getting away from it however, it helps build resilience and character. Ultimately, rejection is just feedback which I covered in Strategy Number 17.

Some people you may know who were rejected before they became successful: J.K. Rowling, Oprah Winfrey, Steve Jobs, Madonna, Bill Gates, Elvis, Michael Jordan and Sylvester (Sly) Stallone to name but some.

When I work with personal clients who feel they have been rejected, we look at the reality of the situation, not the story of what happened and look at other possibilities that may be the real truth. Including the actions of other people involved.

Here's the thing, you will probably not think about how the other person was feeling at the time, and what 'state' they were in. Most of the time, it is the actions of others that you are letting impact your own feelings. Did you know, according to work by Dr David R Hawkins, that 87% of the world population are in a negative state. Therefore, you are letting their actions dictate how you feel potentially robbing you of your confidence.

Your confidence is your driving force and don't let other people's actions rob you of your power to succeed. Rise above it as there are always more opportunities available and more often than not, they are a better alternative anyway.

EXERCISE

Write on a piece of paper and put in a prominent place –

"Rejection is just feedback and another step towards improvement!"

"Don't personalise rejection. Often times the flaw is in the other person."

- Dr Phil

STRATEGY NUMBER 20

BEING REALISTIC

STRATEGY NUMBER 20
BEING REALISTIC

Have you ever wanted to get from A to B quickly however, it seems to take longer than planned?

Everyone has been there! I know I have!!

However, if the goal isn't achieved, most people blame themselves and it can impact confidence massively. As the quote says: *"Most people overestimate what they can do in a day/week/month/year and underestimate what they can do in 10 years"* - Bill Gates

You see, when most goals are set, they don't allow any 'wiggle room'. Hey, if life was perfect and that goal was the only thing to focus on then fair enough however, with life being 'so busy' these days, and with many distractions: emails, mobile phones etc, a bit more realism is required in most cases.

You may well want to jump from A to B for personal reasons and learn a new skill or many skills in a short period of time, however, the thing is, you are improving and getting better all of the time and that alone, should increase your confidence. The realistic goal is not to be perfect but to improve on a daily basis.

Imagine if you improved 1% in something today. *'1% Dave, that is not worth talking about.'* Look, I hear you, and on the surface, you are exactly right so bear with me. Now, imagine you did that daily for the next year. That would equate to being 37% better over the year – wow! A 37% increase is great in most people's book. Imagine that growth in your savings account. Now imagine that growth over 10 years. It is called compounding. Wouldn't it make sense to compound your positive achievements instead of your negative ones?

Now apply that to your confidence and how that is going to increase exponentially and perhaps when you look back at the 'old you' in 10 years, you won't recognise yourself because of your growth.

Imagine this, your goals are like a tree. You start off with your seed and when it is planted, you are on your way. However, it needs food and water for its roots to grow strong otherwise it is going to be very flimsy and easily blown over. Once it is nurtured for the right amount of time, the tree will flourish and grow strong, resulting in an amazing canopy of leaves.

The alternative to that is to force grow your tree which is always possible, however, the tree isn't as tall, the trunk isn't as strong, and the canopy isn't as amazing.

That is the same scenario when you force things without being realistic. They aren't as strong in their outcomes. It is a bit like you wanting a surgeon to operate on your heart without having years of training and practice – you wouldn't want it would you?

The challenge these days is we are in the 'now society' where so many things are wanted immediately. So many things are available to order at their fingertips via their phones or computers.

The reality is, sometimes, we need to let things nurture and develop without forcing them. Realising along the way, that every day, you have grown more, learnt more in readiness for your final outcome.

Because you know you have increased your wins/your skillsets/your successes, they are all going into your positive staking pile to increase your confidence.

EXERCISE

When you are setting a goal, is it realistic and have you given yourself some 'wiggle room'?

Ask yourself 'how have I grown today?' and diarise/journal it for reference.

"Continuous improvement is better than delayed perfection."

- Mark Twain

STRATEGY NUMBER 21

SMILE

STRATEGY NUMBER 21
SMILE

What is a smile?

It is obviously different to many people but in general, people smile because they are happy and when you are happy, you are coming from an emotion of gratitude and love.

Did you know?

There are 43 muscles in the face, most of which are controlled by the cranial nerve (facial nerve). Seventeen of those muscles are used when you smile, and 43 of them are working when you frown.

Now it may seem a good idea to exercise your face and burn more calories by using more muscles by frowning, however, it decreases your state, which impacts your confidence.

Think about it, have you ever smiled at someone, and they have responded in kind, and smiled back? (Well, either that or they thought you were weird for smiling at them :) How did it make you feel?

It helped you feel good, I am sure. It enhanced your state, and you may well have had a bit of a skip in your step knowing you have made someone else feel better about themselves or their current situation.

Have you ever started to watch a film when you really weren't in a good mood? Then you found you really enjoyed it, and you could feel your smile beaming all over your face? How was your mood then?

Smiling is such a simple tool that you have in your armoury, and yet, so powerful for yourself and others. When you impact someone in a good way and it is reciprocated, you can change your state by changing their physiology, and that helps increase your confidence because you feel good.

When I am speaking at an event, smiling is always something we have some fun with. We may well do something outrageous and unexpected that puts a smile on everyone's face, changes their state and opens them up to being more attentive.

When you think about it, entertainers are paid handsomely aren't they? Why? Apart they help change people's mood and enhance their state. So, the audience feel better, possibly go and see them again, or recommend others to see them, and increase revenue, so entertainers are paid handsomely.

Now, I am not saying that you will be paid handsomely financially by smiling at others. But what you can become is rich emotionally, because of the impact you are having on others.

When you are rich emotionally, confidence just flows and impacts everything you do and in a good way. People flock to you and listen to everything you say because of the way you impact them. Because of the impact you have on them, they feel empowered and that is all because of you.

EXERCISE

Smile more and feel the difference!

"A smile is happiness you'll find right under your nose!"

- *Tom Wilson*

STRATEGY NUMBER 22

STOP TRYING TO BE PERFECT

CHAPTER NUMBER 22
STOP TRYING TO BE PERFECT

Most people try their upmost to be perfect, maybe you do too, and the reality is most people are setting themselves up to fail.

That probably sounds harsh I know but if you think about it, perfection is an opinion.

Those opinions are based on people's standards and tragically, many people's standards aren't too high these days. Now I know that doesn't apply to you, as you are an achiever as you wouldn't be reading this book if you weren't.

Have you ever produced a piece of work or done something for someone and not been 100% happy with it? And yet, the feedback you received was absolutely amazing and they may have even used the word perfect in their feedback to you? Yet, you felt it wasn't as good as you wanted it to be?

I know I have. You see, that is the difference in standards. To the recipient, it was much better than they could have done so to them it was perfect so it was their opinion compared to their standards.

The reality is, your terminology of being perfect is giving 100% of your time and effort as you cannot give anymore. You have then produced outstanding work and as close to perfection that you can give, so it is the best of you!

When you know you have given your all and, cannot give any more that will give you the confidence to sit back and admire what you have done.

When you know you have given everything, that will enhance your confidence!

EXERCISE

Again, grab a pen and paper.

Treat yourself like you would a loved one. Make a list of all the things you love and admire about yourself celebrate your better moments. Give yourself encouragement and review this list frequently.

"People always try to be perfect. that is why they don't start anything. perfection is the lowest standard in the world. because if you are trying to be perfect, you know you can't be. So, what you really have is a standard you cannot be. you want to be outstanding and not perfect!"

- Tony Robbins

STRATEGY NUMBER 23

INCANTATIONS

STRATEGY NUMBER 23
INCANTATIONS

According to 75 Media, in the UK, you are exposed to an excess of 5000 advertising messages daily. And they are taking over and impregnating a part of your brain. Don't believe me? Complete the straplines from these companies.........

Nike - Just ....

Red Bull - Gives ....

McDonalds - I'm ....

L'Oreal - Because ....

I bet you managed to complete the straplines or some of them anyway, didn't you?

The reality is, most of us can. That is the advertiser's job, to get into your conscious and other than conscious mind so their product is dormant waiting there. In effect, because you see the adverts or images so frequently, even more impactful when there is a tune you know and associate to the item, you incant them to your mind. You normally don't think of the product or item most of the time until, it comes into a conversation, or you consciously think of a product.

Let me as you a question? If I was to say training shoe, and who do you think of first? Most people will say Nike. What is the difference between Nike and say Adidas? Not a lot really as their shoes do the same job, it is just for many, the Nike adverts resonated more.

Here's the thing, I bet you don't send an annual invoice to those organisations for your minds rental space, do you?

How is it that you remember the adverts, even if, you haven't seen them for a while?

Repetition is the mother of all skills and the more you see and hear something then the easier it is to remember. In other words, you incant it further into your mind.

The reality is the same psychology applies to things that are impacting your confidence as well. News, negative comments, poor self-communication etc.

That pattern needs to be broken and that is where incantations come in. This is not just positive self-talk. These are affirmations, or incantations, that will impact your whole body. They are statements done in a certain way that you can use anytime to give yourself a boost, so you are primed with your confidence.

I referred to affirmations/incantations with a previous strategy as you are using them more than you think. So why not use them to YOUR advantage?

These incantations can be done anywhere at any time and a strategy I suggest when I am working with clients is to do them in the shower. Why? Most people shower on a daily basis, and it is something you know you do daily, like brushing your teeth. Showering, brushing your teeth is something that is done daily for most people, so doing your incantations at the same time becomes habitual over time. It doesn't have to be in the shower as sometimes, my clients do them when they are exercising, maximising their time.

The real key to incantations is to say them out loud with intensity, using a beat and changing the inflections of what you are saying.

A well known example would be:
Every day, in every way, I am getting strong and stronger
Every day, in every way, I am getting wealthier and wealthier
Every day, in every way, I am getting fitter and fitter
Every day, in every way, I am getting healthier and healthier

Now, I am sure that as you are reading those you are imagining a beat to go with them. If so, that is great as the body responds to rhythm and when you do these incantations, on a regular basis, with belief, meaning and intensity, you are reprogramming your mind.

As simple as it sounds, it works and helps change your state and confidence!

N.B. Because I am looking to help you improve your confidence, I don't want you to feel stuck with the advertising straplines I mentioned earlier so here are the answers:

Nike – 'Just DO IT'
Red Bull – 'Gives YOU WINGS'
McDonalds – 'I'm LOVIN' IT'
L'Oreal – 'Because I'M WORTH IT'

So how did you get on? Whatever your score, put that in your confidence stacking pile.

EXERCISE

Design your own affirmations/incantations, and rhythm, you can use daily to empower yourself, anytime, anywhere, and have some fun when you are doing it.

Then anchor it in with the move you created with Strategy Number 5, being in a Peak State.

"Never say anything about yourself you don't want to come true."

- Brian Tracy

ONE LAST MESSAGE

CONGRATULATIONS!

I am proud of you for making the great decision to better yourself by reading the strategies, stories and completing the exercises in this book.

My mission with this book was to serve you and make a positive difference in your life by inspiring you to think and act differently.

My hope, is that you have become more inspired and empowered to BE MORE, DO MORE and ACHIEVE MORE.

Whether you achieve your dreams and goals is solely up to you. No one can promise or guarantee what level of success you will achieve.

However, by following simple success strategies like those in this book, YOU CAN begin to accomplish anything you desire.

YOU CAN DO IT - THE TIME TO START IS NOW!

Again, congratulations.

"The best time to plant a tree
was 20 years ago. The
second best time is
NOW!"
- *Chinese Proverb*

ACKNOWLEDGEMENTS

Through the years, many have shared ideas, mentoring and support that has impacted my life, each in a different way. It's impossible to thank everyone and I apologise for anyone not listed. Please know, that I appreciate you greatly. Big love, always.

It goes without saying to start with my mum and dad! Julie and Brian Malyon, Ann Parry, Jane and Peter Morgan, Paula Wollaston, Helen and Adrian Hughes, Matt Windsor, Rachel Moore, Nicki Young, Ian and Mandy Smith, Wayne and Mandy Goodwin, Santosh and Bahader Bahra, Lucy and Scott Williams, Julie and Doug, Graham Pickering, Pascale Holden, Dean and Karen Ward, Darren Sheppard, Darren Bradley, Sam Pearce, Jo 'Digger' Barnes, Jan Wilson, Marie & John Malyon, Karen Shore, Loraine Thomas, Marcella Lord, Guy McMillan, Nicky J Davies, Pam and Brian Budd, Poonam Sandhar, Ron Lawrence, Sarah Cox, Dorinda Jarmain, Richard Howlett, Stacey Power, Tina Bhudia, Tony and Gerry Mears, Yvette Hoye, Sally Hames, Sue & Jimbo Bartlett, Julie D'Ann, Shiran Cohen, David Bevan and Jane Clark, Sally Hull, David Forbes and Lisa Forrest, Brian Thomas, Dave Nunn, Michael Butler, Chris and Penny Pooley, Lynne Richardson, Richard Tissington, Helene Hazell, Lee Meakin, Stephen Wells, Steve Cartwright, Steve and Bev Baxter, Salsabila Al-Harby, Josh Harrington, Dave L Tree and Denyse Jones, Neil 'Oggy' Ogden, Lisa Zevi, Pilar Karlen, Pinder and Bobsy Gill, Abid Hussein, Marie Oldfield, Josh Harrington, Tony Robbins, Dean Graziosi, Andy Harrington, Cheryl Chapman, Ruth Driscoll, James Lavers, Matt Elwell, Tony and Nicky Vee, Jack Duggan, Kate and Stuart Guest, Kerrie Atherton, Dave Bola, Di Noonan, Marion Bevington, Kerry Bartley, Martin Sharpe, Nigel Irving, James Malinchak, Nick James, Dr David Heber, Louis Ignarro, Ian Pathryjohns, Dr Luigi Gratton, James Stoner, Adele-Marie Hartshorn, Laura Tynan, Ryan Mathie, Sai Blackbyrn, Karissa Kouchis, Danny Bahra, Nick & Megan Unsworth, Manny Bahra, Dee Pattni, Ricky Bahra, Katie Smith, Kim & Nick Lewis & Dot Warren, Julie & Kevin Unsworth, Eleri & Andy Hodgson, Bosco Bonilla, Ant Hodges, Yvonne Dales & Dave Bola.

About Dave

Dave Williams is an award winning coach and trainer with his personal clients and many well known organisations. Having been described as 'our secret weapon' by one organisation. Helping personal clients including: directors, managers, athletes, overcome their 'blockages' and increase their confidence.

Assisting businesses increase their turnover, and improving their leadership and management development.

www.davewilliamscoaching.com

Dave is an inspirational speaker who has now spoken in 4 different continents. Being described by one client as 'the best guest speaker we have ever had.' His talks are interactive and fun. His main deliverable subjects are about mindset, management and mental health. As a coach, he doesn't just talk, he gives people practical solutions to take away and implement to improve their lives.

www.switchonthelightcoach.co.uk

ADDITIONAL RESOURCES

The W.I.N. to Live Roadmap ™

Take YOUR Confidence to another level with this home study course.

WWW.W2LIVEROADMAP.CO.UK

The Management M.A.S.T.E.R.Y. University ™

Take YOUR management skills to the next level and perform at your peak for outstanding results, personally and in your business!

WWW.MANAGEMENTMASTERYUNIVERSITY.COM

Special <u>FREE</u> Bonus Gift For You

To help you achieve more success, there are
FREE BONUS RESOURCES for you at:

www.FreeGiftFromDave.info

- 4 In-depth training videos on how to improve your confidence to help you achieve more goals and greater success

"I believe when you were born, you were like a fantastic, perfect diamond, beautiful in every way.

Some great experiences in your life made those cuts shine so brilliantly; the light just sparkles like a star in the sky.

However, some of your life's experiences have not been so good and cloak these beautiful cuts so they have been dimmed or they don't sparkle at all.

The beauty of life is you can change how you view your experiences and polish your diamond. So, you can shine for the whole world to see the magnificent person you really are.

And YOU have the power to 'switch on your light' at any time!"

- Dave Williams

Printed in Great Britain
by Amazon

22480117R00079